Can I tell you about Asperger Syndrome?

also by Jude Welton

What Did You Say? What Do You Mean?
An Illustrated Guide to Understanding Metaphors
Jude Welton and Jane Telford
ISBN 978 1 84310 207 6

Adam's Alternative Sports Day
An Asperger Story
ISBN 978 184310 300 4

of related interest

My Social Stories Book
Carol Gray and Abbie Leigh White
Illustrated by Sean McAndrew
ISBN 978 185302 950 9

Asperger's Syndrome
A Guide for Parents and Professionals
Tony Attwood
ISBN 978 185302 577 8

Freaks, Geeks and Asperger Syndrome
A User Guide to Adolescence
Luke Jackson
ISBN 978 184310 098 0

Can I tell you about Asperger Syndrome?
A guide for friends and family

Jude Welton

Illustrated by Jane Telford

Foreword by Elizabeth Newson

Jessica Kingsley Publishers
London and Philadelphia

First published in the United Kingdom in 2004
by Jessica Kingsley Publishers
116 Pentonville Road
London N1 9JB, UK
and
400 Market Street, Suite 400
Philadelphia, PA 19106, USA

www.jkp.com

Text copyright © Jude Welton 2004
Illustrations copyright © Jane Telford 2004

Library of Congress Cataloging in Publication Data

Welton, Jude, 1955-
  Can I tell you about Asperger syndrome? : a guide for friends and
family / Jude Welton ; illustrated by Jane Telford ; foreword by
Elizabeth Newson.— 1st American pbk. ed.
     v. cm.
  Includes bibliographical references.
  Contents: Introducing Adam, who has Asperger syndrome — Reading
feelings — Tones of voice — Playing with others — Loud noises —
Confusing groups — Unexpected change — Motor skills — Special
interests — What is Asperger syndrome?
   ISBN 1-84310-206-4 (pbk.)
  1. Asperger's syndrome—Juvenile literature. [1. Asperger's syndrome.
2. Autism.] I. Title.
   RJ506.A9W44 2004
   618.92'8588—dc22
                                                      2003027296

British Library Cataloguing in Publication Data
A CIP catalogue record for this book is available from the British Library

ISBN 978 1 84310 206 9

Printed and Bound in Great Britain by
Athenaeum Press, Gateshead, Tyne and Wear

To the special children at Dyke Primary School
who live up to their school motto "Think of Others"

and to their special head teacher, Ian MacKay

Contents

Acknowledgements

I would like to thank Elizabeth Newson, who first introduced me to the world of autism many years ago. A student couldn't ask for a more inspiring, sympathetic teacher. And when autism touched my life more closely than I could have expected, Elizabeth remained an equally inspiring and sympathetic friend, mentor and advocate. Her encouragement and suggestions gave me the confidence to see this book through to its completion.

Thanks too to Eileen Griffith, my son's educational psychologist, for her comments and suggestions, and for the unfailing support she gives children with autistic spectrum disorders in our area. I'd like to thank Carol Gray, whose Social Stories have taught me so much, and which continue to help my son. And special thanks go to "the other Carol Gray", who has supported my son at school with such sensitivity and devotion. Indeed, thanks go to all the staff and children at Dyke Primary School for their understanding, patience and care.

Thanks to Jane for the wonderful illustrations, and to Joyce Mason for her creative ideas. Many thanks go to my family for their loving support and understanding. Thanks too to Jessica for saying "yes", and to everyone at JKP for all their help.

But most of all I'd like to say thank you to my husband David, and to JJ, our lovely son, who inspired this book.

Foreword

The beginning of the 21st century has seen an explosion in the recognition and diagnosis of Asperger Syndrome (and probably also in its actual incidence). Along with this higher profile among clinicians, parents and the media, has come a determination among young people with Asperger's both to understand themselves more fully, and to make sure that other people not only are aware of their difficulties but appreciate their special qualities and talents.

One of those talents being a facility with computers, it is hardly surprising that many of the early exchanges of views and information among people with Asperger's emerged via the internet, and the computer revolution has undoubtedly been an important source of self-esteem for adults with Asperger Syndrome, who have increasingly contributed to scientific debate from the inside. However, of equal interest to clinicians who listen to the children has been their capacity to consider their own condition and what it means to them, often at a surprisingly early age.

We came to this by way of workshops for brothers and sisters, where we had identified seven years as a realistic age for "explaining" their sibling's condition satisfactorily – but of course these children had good social empathy. I had started experimenting with writing letters to adolescents with Asperger's (following clinical sessions), which was promising. It was really when I suggested to Edward's parents that (at nine or ten) he might soon enjoy reading bits of Marc Segar's brilliant insider's book "Coping", that their reply ("He's already read a lot of it") made me start to include seven-year-old children with Asperger's in my explanatory letters.

Glenys Jones's optimistic review of research on various projects designed to help young people to understand (and so take ownership of) their Asperger Syndrome confirmed me in the belief that the sensitive sharing of information can be therapeutic for the person most intimately involved, just as it is for parents and siblings. I was still more convinced by a nine-year-old who, on the way to his diagnostic assessment, told his parents that his biggest worry was: "Suppose she doesn't know what's wrong with me?"; he needed an explanation of Asperger's before he went home that day, and insisted that his mother frame and put up on his bedroom wall the letter that I eventually wrote for him.

Jude Welton, who would probably not have written this book if she had not seen from the inside her own child's need of it, has potentially extended the scope for sharing the diagnosis, by giving the young child with Asperger's the power of his own voice in explaining himself to his friends. Her calm and deceptively simple approach is complemented by Jane Telford's reassuringly everyday pictures.

Parents have needed this book for a very long time, and the rest of the family will find it a welcome introduction to the enigma that is Asperger's. It will also be especially helpful to primary schools, who would love to establish a "Circle of Friends" for a child with Asperger's if only they could be sure how well he under-stood himself: clearly, one cannot explain the child to a circle of his peers if he himself is not already within the loop of information. That this book has made the child himself the source of his friends' knowledge is its particular strength.

Elizabeth Newson
Early Years Diagnostic Centre, Nottingham

This book has been written for boys and girls aged about 7–15 years old to help them to understand the difficulties faced by a child with Asperger Syndrome (AS). It tells them what AS is, what it feels like to have AS, and how they can help. It is also a useful, friendly book to share with children who have recently had their own diagnosis of AS explained to them.

"I usually call it AS for short.
I'd like to tell you what it is, what it
feels like, and how you might help me –
if you want to."

"You can't see that I have Asperger Syndrome. I look like most other boys. But you might notice things about me that are a bit different. This is because AS can make me behave and talk a bit differently from the way you might expect. Like everyone else, people with AS are individuals, and AS affects each person a bit differently. So other children with AS will be like me in lots of ways, but not exactly the same.

Having AS means that I have certain talents and certain difficulties. I have a very good memory for example, and know lots of information about subjects that interest me. I'm good at maths, and the computer, and I know lots of facts about things like dinosaurs, football clubs, trains and birds.

But having AS means I have difficulties with some things that most people don't have trouble with. My main difficulties are with what some people call 'social sense' – understanding and getting along with other people easily."

"I find it hard to understand
the expressions on people's faces.
So it's difficult for me
to know how they are feeling."

"**M**ost people don't realize it, but they **naturally** know a lot about what other people are feeling and thinking. Most people can understand 'body language' – expressions, gestures and body movements that give information about the way people feel and think, and what they are intending to do and why. It's as if they can 'read' feelings by looking at someone's face and seeing the expression in his or her eyes. They can 'hear' feelings in the way a person talks. This is sometimes called 'tuning in' to other people. Most people don't have to be taught how to 'tune in'. They just do it naturally.

But I find it very hard to understand body language, and to know what someone else might be thinking or feeling. It doesn't come naturally to me, and I have to be taught how to do it.

You might notice that I sometimes look away from you, so that I don't have to look you in the eye. This doesn't mean I'm not listening to you, or that I mean to be unfriendly. It's just that looking people in the eye can sometimes make me feel confused and uncomfortable."

"Although I understand the **words** people say, I often find it difficult to make sense of the tone of their voice."

"Sometimes I can get confused if people say things sarcastically. Like if someone says 'That's great!', meaning the opposite. I can also find things like metaphors – such as 'Pull your socks up' – confusing. I have a similar problem with jokes.

This is because people with AS think literally, and expect words to mean what they say. You can help me by being kind if I misunderstand something you've said, and maybe by explaining a joke or a metaphor if I don't get it.

I also find it very difficult to tell if someone is talking or acting in a **friendly** teasing way or a **bullying** teasing way. Other people can usually tell the difference, but I usually can't. This can make me feel very stressed, and I might get upset and angry because I think you're being unfriendly when you're really not.

I can understand lots of things that some people can't (like maths and computers and history). But please try to understand that I **can't** always make sense of some things that might be obvious to you! And if I'm feeling confused or stressed, I might say or do something that upsets you without meaning to. Please let me know if I do that."

"I sometimes find it difficult to play games happily with other children."

"**N**ot being able to tune in naturally to other people can make it difficult for me to take turns, or to play cooperatively. If I feel confused about what people are doing, or what I am expected to do, I might be afraid to join in with games even if I do want to be friendly. Sometimes things seem to go too fast for me, and I feel muddled about what to do.

I might only want to play if I decide on the game, and choose the rules. This isn't just me being bossy. It's because I feel safer and less confused if I make the rules.

You could help me by gently reminding me about taking turns, and by taking a bit of extra time to explain the rules of the games you are playing.

Also, please understand that I sometimes need to play quietly on my own. The world can seem very noisy and confusing when you have AS, and I sometimes just need to be by myself, and chill out on my own."

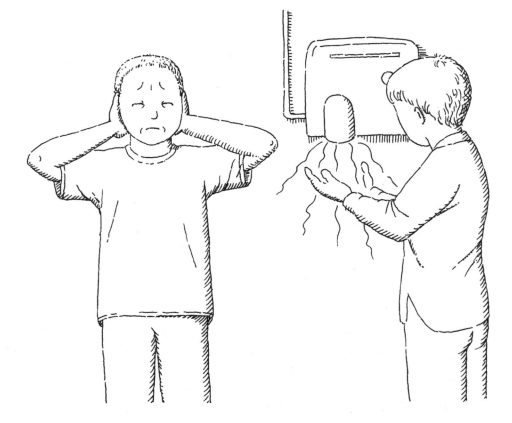

"Loud noises can feel painful to me."

"Most people with AS have what are called 'sensory' problems – they may be very sensitive to what they taste, touch, smell, see or hear. But these difficulties aren't exactly the same for everyone. Having AS affects everyone a bit differently.

Some people might absolutely hate the touch of certain materials against their skin. Others feel pain in an unusual way – some find light touches painful, for example, while others don't feel pain when most people would. Some people with AS might find it difficult to cope with certain smells, tastes or textures of food. With me, it's noises that can cause the biggest problems.

If I'm in a room or a shop with lots of people making a noise, or if I'm in a crowded playground, or if people speak loudly and quickly to me, I can feel overwhelmed and panicky. Also, if there is a sudden loud noise such as a hand dryer, it can really hurt my ears. Sometimes I cover my ears to block out the painful, confusing sounds, and just want to run away.

You can help me by not making sudden loud noises, and by being understanding if I am upset by being in noisy places."

"I often find being with a group of children stressful and confusing. This can make me feel angry, and can make me behave in what seems like an unfriendly way."

"**I** usually feel most comfortable with one person I know and like. I sometimes misunderstand what people are doing and why they are doing it, especially if I'm in a group. This can make me feel very stressed out.

If I'm confused about what people are doing, I can get frustrated and angry, and might do or say things that seem unfriendly. But I'm not really meaning to be unfriendly: it's usually because I feel uncomfortable and muddled.

And sometimes I just feel overwhelmed by all the noise and sights around me. If I meet lots of new people at once, I can't always tell their faces apart, and that's confusing. If the classroom is noisy, I find it really difficult to concentrate, and don't always notice if someone talks to me. I don't mean to be rude.

Most people can filter out sounds or sights or smells, but because I have AS, I can't always do that. Sometimes I feel overloaded with all this input, and I need to be somewhere quiet and peaceful to help me calm down."

"I can get very upset when unexpected things happen, or when there's a change of plan that I haven't been warned about."

"For people like me who have AS, the world can feel like a confusing place that doesn't always make sense. Routines – things that always happen in the same way or in the same order – can be very comforting and help make me feel safe. Routines let me know what is going to happen. I like that. Change means things can happen that I'm not expecting, and I find that difficult to cope with.

Change is actually much easier to cope with if I'm prepared for it. So if we plan to do something together, and you need to change the plan, please let me know in advance. Then I can be ready for it. People with AS don't usually like surprises.

However, doing new things can be fun. As long as I'm prepared for a new experience, and I've been told exactly what's expected of me and what's going to happen, I'm usually keen to try. If someone can write down what's going to happen, rather than just tell me, it really helps."

"Sometimes I feel really frustrated
and fed up because my arms aren't
as strong as I wish they were."

"People with AS often have some problems with 'motor skills', which means they can't always control and coordinate their body movements as well as they would like to. They might be a bit clumsy, or have problems catching or kicking a ball, or copying people's movements in a dance or martial arts class.

With me, the main problem is that my shoulders and arms aren't very strong, which makes some things like swinging on monkey bars difficult. But I do lots of exercises that help, and I'm gradually getting stronger and more coordinated.

You can help by being sympathetic if I find things like sport difficult, and by being patient if you're showing me how to do something. I might need you to show me slowly, and more than once.

If you're showing me how to make a physical movement, it can help if you don't face towards me, but face the same way, standing beside or in front of me. Then I usually find it easier to copy movements. It might help if we both do it facing a long mirror."

"I'm happy and relaxed when I'm involved with my special interests. I'm really into computers and dinosaurs."

"Most people with AS have special interests – subjects that interest them more than anything else. Other people with AS might have different special interests from me, for example stars or trains or motor racing. When I'm doing something on my computer or reading or writing about dinosaurs, I feel very happy and relaxed, and I find it really easy to concentrate and focus.

Sometimes, I forget that not everyone shares my interests and I might want to talk about them too much. So if I do go on about dinosaurs for example, I might need help to change the subject. Please be patient. It makes me feel safe and confident to talk about things I know a lot about. But you might have to remind me that you'd like to talk about something else. I might not be able to 'read' your face and know if you're bored.

When people with AS grow up, they might become experts in their special interests. Like me, some computer experts have been into computers since they were children. Some of them have AS too."

"Why is it called Asperger Syndrome?
Is it an illness?
Will you always have it?"

"It's named after a doctor called Hans Asperger who worked with children in the 1940s. It's not an illness. It's a type of autism, which is a condition that affects the way the brain processes information.

Having this type of autism means my brain is very good at processing some sorts of information, such as facts and figures, but has difficulty processing the sort of information that helps make sense of what other people are thinking, feeling and communicating. Both boys and girls can have AS, but it affects more boys than girls.

No one knows exactly why people have AS. It's something some people are born with, but it isn't usually noticed until they are a bit older. I will always have AS, but as I grow up, I can come to learn most of what comes naturally to most people. With the help of friends and grown-ups, AS can get much easier to cope with.

Having AS does have advantages. People with AS are often original thinkers, and can become experts in the subjects that most interest them. Some famous scientists and artists, such as Albert Einstein and L.S. Lowry, are thought to have had AS. You never know, I might become a world expert on dinosaurs one day, or develop a whole new computer language!"

"The main way you can help is by realizing that I have AS, and being sympathetic."

"Please invite me to join in – but understand that I can find being in a group stressful. I'm not being unfriendly if I sometimes prefer to be on my own.

- Please don't speak too quickly. If you do, I can't always take in everything you say.

- Please take time to explain the rules of games.

- I might need help to take turns. Let me know if I have to wait my turn, but please try to be patient.

- Try not to get cross if I misunderstand you.

- I don't always realize if I've said or done something upsetting or a bit silly. So you may have to tell me if I've upset you.

- Please remember that I usually take things literally. I might not understand metaphors, jokes or sarcasm.

- If possible, let me know in advance if there is a change in plan, so that I can be ready for it.

- I have very sensitive hearing, so please don't shout or make loud sudden noises unexpectedly. Remember, other people with AS may have other problems with hearing, touch, taste or smell or with things like bright lights.

Try to understand that although I want friends, I don't always know how to behave in a friendly way. I need you to be patient and friendly and supportive. I'll try to be the same for you!"

How Teachers Can Help

UNDERSTANDING WHAT MAKES ME STRESSED

"Please be aware that I find lots of things at school very stressful and difficult to cope with. Examples are:

- Choices. I find deciding between one option and another very stressful.

- Background noise. It's difficult for me to filter out and ignore background noise. This can make concentrating difficult, and can make me feel stressed.

- Loud, sudden noises – from hand dryers to fire alarms. Raised voices can make me panic.

- Some children with AS find school strip lights very uncomfortable, especially if they flicker. And sometimes the writing on notices or the board seems to move about, so it's really hard to read it properly.

- Unexpected things. Please give me advance notice about changes, or things that don't usually happen - anything from a change in timetable, to a different teacher from usual.

- If I misunderstand what people want of me, or make some other mistake, it can make me feel very stressed and stupid. Social Stories have helped me with this.

- Break times. There's no structure, and I don't always know what to do. I may need help playing with other children. Perhaps someone could teach me some playground games, so that I know how to join in. Sometimes, though, I may need to be on my own for a bit. Lunch times are also difficult, mainly because of the noise."

REDUCING STRESS

"There are some simple things that can make a big difference in helping me to feel less stressed and more able to cope in school. For example:

- Please give me a timetable so that I can keep track of what's happening and when in the school day. I feel stressed and worried otherwise. I can't usually remember just by being told. I need to see it. When I was younger I had a visual timetable with icons, but now that I'm older, a written timetable works well for me.

- Altering the icons on the visual timetable, or noting the change on the written timetable, helps me prepare for and cope with changes.

- It helps if I have a 'Quiet Corner' or some other quiet place to go to when I need a break, because I sometimes get overloaded with stress and the noise of the classroom. Also, knowing that I have a break coming up once I've completed work can help me to get my work done.

- Some work sheets look so cluttered with information that it makes me feel muddled and flustered. It can sometimes help if the teacher makes the work sheets look less cluttered, perhaps by covering up some examples.

- Please teach me techniques to reduce my anxiety. Being taught relaxation techniques such as breathing exercises or foot massage can really help."

TALKING AND LISTENING

"Please be aware that the way you speak affects how much I can take in. Also, please understand that I may appear not to be paying attention when I am.

- If you speak quickly, I can't usually keep up with what you say. Speaking quite slowly, and pausing between sentences helps.

- If you don't say my name at the beginning of a sentence, I might not realize that you are talking to me – especially if I am in a group. I'm not deliberately ignoring you if I don't respond. If you only say my name at the end of a sentence, I may miss the sentence altogether. "Adam, please pass me the book" is better for me than "Please pass me the book, Adam".

- Some children with AS may listen better when they are not looking at the teacher.[*] Sometimes I feel overloaded with the information coming in through my eyes and ears. Then I might need to listen, but not look. I'm not meaning to be rude. At that time, this may be the only way for me to pay attention to what you are saying.

- Please explain yourself clearly. For example, if you say "tidy up", I might not know what to do. If you want me to collect papers and put them in a tray, please say so.

- Like most people with AS, I learn best when I can **see** what you mean. Rather than just talking, if you write things down, or draw pictures or diagrams to explain things, it helps me to understand and remember."

SPECIAL DIFFICULTIES

"Here are some other special difficulties that can affect how well I get on at school:

- If I find a topic difficult or boring, I might get upset or want to give up on it. Being motivated to do things you don't want to do can be a real problem when you have AS. Social Stories, stickers and rewards can help. It can also help if teachers try to find some link with my special interest – or let me

---

[*]   Author's note: Recent research has shown that this can be true of other children too.

spend some time on my special interest as a reward for working on the set topic.

- Occasionally, some subject matter might make me very anxious, and I may feel unable to cope with learning about it in class or even watching a video about it. Please be understanding if this happens.

- Like many children with AS, I have problems with motor skills. I find handwriting and some sport difficult, and need extra help and understanding. For some children, it helps to have lines to write on.

- I have a lot of trouble organising myself and my work. You could help by giving me checklists to remind me what to do and in what order. Examples are getting changed for PE, packing my school bag, and organising class work and homework.

- Having AS means that as well as learning the usual subjects, I need help to learn to understand other people and how to behave with them. Social Stories and comic strip conversations help me to make sense of social situations. Social skills groups can also help. Please realize that special help with social stuff can make a huge difference to how well I can cope, and go on coping as I grow up. Thank you!"

Recommended reading, websites and organizations

If you would like to find out more about Asperger Syndrome, here are some useful books, websites and organizations. Several of the books are written by people with AS.

BOOKS

Non-fiction for children and teenagers

Hall, Kenneth (2001) "Asperger Syndrome, The Universe and Everything." London: Jessica Kingsley Publishers.

Jackson, Luke (2002) "Freaks, Geeks and Asperger Syndrome: A User Guide to Adolescence." London: Jessica Kingsley Publishers.

Both these fascinating books are written by boys with AS, and tell you what it's like from the inside.

Faherty, Catherine (2000) "Asperger's: What Does It Mean To Me?" Arlington, TX: Future Horizons.

A work-book for children with AS, teaching self-awareness and life lessons, along with structured teaching ideas for home and school. A really valuable resource.

Fiction for children

Kathy Hoopmann has written a number of books for children which feature children with AS as the heroes. They include:

Hoopmann, Kathy (2000) "Blue Bottle Mystery: An Asperger Adventure." London: Jessica Kingsley Publishers.

Hoopmann, Kathy (2002) "Lisa and the Lacemaker: An Asperger Adventure." London: Jessica Kingsley Publishers.

For older readers

Holliday Willey, Liane (1999) "Pretending to be Normal: Living with Asperger's Syndrome." London: Jessica Kingsley Publishers.

Holliday Willey, Liane (2001) "Asperger Syndrome in the Family: Redefining Normal." London: Jessica Kingsley Publishers.

These two books are by Liane Holliday Willey, a doctor of education, a writer and researcher. Both she and her daughter have AS, and the books give remarkable insights and practical ideas.

Pyles, Lise (2002) "Hitchhiking through Asperger Syndrome: How to Help Your Child When No One Else Will." London: Jessica Kingsley Publishers.

Written by the mother of a child with AS, primarily for other parents. It's inspiring, informative and full of good advice.

Attwood, Tony (1998) "Asperger's Syndrome: A Guide for Parents and Professionals." London: Jessica Kingsley Publishers.

The classic text on AS.

WEBSITES

OASIS
This stands for Online Asperger Information and Support.

www.udel.edu/bkirby/asperger

OASIS was set up in 1995 by Barbara Kirby, a mother of a child with AS. She was later joined by Patricia Romanowski Bashe, who also has a child with AS. Together they have written "The OASIS Guide to Asperger Syndrome" (2001) New York: Crown Publishers. It's an invaluable source of information, advice, inspiration and support.

Tony Attwood
The homepage of Tony Attwood (see "Books" above).

www.tonyattwood.com

ORGANIZATIONS

UK

National Autistic Society
393 City Road
London
EC1V 1NE
website: www.nas.org.uk
email: nas@nas.org.uk
phone: ++44 (0) 207 8332299

USA

Asperger Syndrome Coalition of the US (ASC-US)
2020 Pennsylvania Ave, NW
Box 771
Washington DC 20006
website: www.asperger.org
phone: ++1 (1) 866 4277747

Autism Society of America
7910 Woodmont Avenue, Suite 300
Bethesda
MD 20814-3067
website: www.autism-society.org
email: info@autism-society.org
phone: ++1 (1) 301 6570881

Canada

Aspergers Society of Ontario
293 Wychwood Avenue
Toronto
Ontario
M6C 2T6
website: www.aspergers.ca
email: info@aspergers.ca
phone: ++1 (1) 416 6514037

Australia

Asperger's Syndrome Support Network (Queensland) Inc
PO Box 159
Virginia
QLD 4014
website: www.asperger.asn.au
email: office@asperger.asn.au
phone: ++61 (0) 738 652911

Asperger's Syndrome Support Network
The Nerve Centre
54 Railway Road
Blackburn VIC
email: assnvic@mssociety.com.au
phone: ++61 (0) 398 452766

New Zealand

Autistic Association of New Zealand
PO Box 7035
Sydenham
Christchurch
website: www.autismnz.org.nz
email: info@autismnz.org.nz
phone: ++64 (0) 333 21038

BLANK, FOR YOUR NOTES